Europe
and the
Environment

Europe
and the
Environment

The European Community and
Environmental Policy

**Alison
Press**
    and
**Catherine
Taylor**

The Industrial Society

First published February 1990 by
The Industrial Society
Robert Hyde House
48 Bryanston Square
London W1H 7LN
Tel: 01-262 2401

ISBN 0 85290 471 1

© Alison Press and Catherine Taylor

British Library Cataloguing in Publication Data
Taylor, Catherine
  Europe and the environment: 1992 guide.
  1. European Community countries. Environment. Policies of
  European Economic Community
  I. Title   II. Press, Alison
  333.7094

Typeset by Ace Filmsetting Ltd, Frome, Somerset
Printed and bound in Great Britain by
Bourne Press Limited, Dorset

Contents

Foreword

In the 1990s, Britain will be part of an integrated Europe where 'green' issues will receive unprecedented attention. Indeed, the European Commission is already taking a strong stand in areas such as water and air pollution and waste disposal. The Commission, in adopting a vigorous environmental policy, is responding to the concerns of a united European people for better working and living conditions, and a healthier environment for all.

This must be right. In the end, it is people who matter, and no industrial or commercial venture will ever succeed without the commitment of a healthy and contented workforce.

In *Europe and the Environment*, the authors describe the Commission's role in environmental issues, highlighting key areas of concern and looking at potential remedies. It is a slim volume, but the content is of paramount importance to us all.

Introduction

There is an unprecedented urgency for this generation to support and promote the well-being of our environment actively. The environment is our most valuable asset and all share the responsibility to contain its deterioration.

Environmental concerns are gaining increasing prominence in the political and economic agenda. For example, Margaret Thatcher's address to the United Nations General Assembly stressed that it is no longer viable to squabble over who is responsible or who should pay for environmental deterioration; national and international action needs to be taken now.

This book introduces the European Commission's role in international response to environmental issues and highlights key areas of concern. It looks not only at causes of pollution, such as harmful emissions, but also at potential remedies that the European Commission is initiating and supporting.

This is the second book in the 1992 Series, following *1992: The Facts and Challenges*.

1 Why the EC is involved

Commitment to improving living and working conditions

The European Communities (EC) were founded in 1957 when six European countries signed the Treaty of Rome, which remains the cornerstone of the EC today. One of the fundamental principles laid down in this Treaty was a commitment to improve the living and working conditions of all the peoples of Europe. The cleanliness of our water, for example, affects how we live and work, and thus is a relevant issue to be tackled by the EC.

Commitment to an internal market

In order to complete the Single European Market, companies across Europe must be able to compete on equal terms. This means that Member States must have similar anti-pollution requirements, controls and penalties so that companies face similar costs wherever they are in Europe.

Economic prosperity

It is only recently that the developed world has recognised that short-term economic prosperity is not always consistent with long-term growth and conservation of our natural resources and the protection of our environment. Most of the world's power is derived from relatively scarce natural resources such as coal, oil and gas, in comparison with the amount of power derived from wind, wave or air. Therefore, for companies to be successful, both now and in the future, oil and gas resources have to be managed with care. Global warming largely due to the 'greenhouse effect' – a result of the build-up of CO_2 in the Earth's atmosphere – has attracted recent international concern. This is perhaps evidence that our Earth's resources may not be safe in our hands. Further evidence is the current EC farm support policies which have encouraged maximisation of production leading to industrial farming, irrespective of demand.

International boundaries

The detrimental effects of pollution are not constricted by borders. For example, acid rain stemming from factory emissions from all over Europe, including the UK, is depleting the forests in Scandinavia and is causing erosion of historical buildings in West Germany. Given that the EC is a geographic grouping and Member States share natural features such as rivers and seas, preventative action to conserve these has to be taken at the European level. However, the European response in isolation is not sufficient as ultimately the problems are international and will also have to be tackled at a global level.

Responsiveness to the people of Europe

Public awareness of environmental issues has been growing in the last 30 years, at both a national and a Community level. This is not only reflected in the increasing demand for environmentally sound consumer products and services, such as detergents and bottle banks; political representation is also increasing. The results of the

1989 European Elections demonstrate the strength of feeling that Europeans have about their deteriorating environment and the more general growth of the environmental movement. In the UK alone, the Green party received about 15 per cent of the vote in these elections. As a representative body of all Member States, the European Commission has a duty to co-ordinate and initiate action in response to this growing concern.

2 How the EC is involved

Concern about the environment is not new. Issues such as the depletion of natural resources were clearly recognised as early as the 1950s; by the 1970s, industrialised countries were beginning to take co-ordinated action. The 1972 United Nations conference on the Environment was rapidly followed by a European Community response; in October 1972, EC Heads of State concluded that economic expansion was not an end in itself. This led to the following Community principles for the development of an environmental policy:

- prevention is better than cure; the sources of pollution need to be tackled rather than the symptoms
- in order to be effective any environmental policy has to be compatible with economic and social development
- planning and decision making at all levels must take into account its effects on the environment from the outset
- significant damage to the ecological balance caused by, for example, over-exploitation of natural resources must be avoided
- polluters must bear the cost of preventing and eliminating detrimental actions. This 'polluters pay' principle is still at the fore of the Commission's mind in disaster recoveries
- the Community must increase its level of scientific and technological understanding of environmental issues and their impacts. Research work must, therefore, be encouraged
- each Member State has a responsibility to the others in terms of protecting the environment
- the Community as a whole has to take into account the effects of its environmental policy on developing countries
- the Community and Member States have a responsibility in

lobbying and contributing to international environmental organisations
- protecting the environment concerns all in the Community – so raising awareness is vital
- specific levels of action must be developed for each different type of pollution
- environmental policy can no longer be developed on a national basis in isolation from other Member States
- Community environmental policy should not, however, hamper national policy but rather co-ordinate and harmonise Member States' actions. These actions, in turn, must be compatible with a Single Market.

Since these principles were developed, the Community has undertaken a series of environmental action programmes, each lasting four years, to tackle the problems in the natural as well as the man-made environment.

These aim to :

- keep pollution to a minimum and where possible eliminate it entirely
- maintain the ecological balance of the environment
- avoid exploitation of natural resources
- pursue economic development within defined quality standards for living
- plan urban development with environmental issues in mind
- participate in finding international solutions to environmental problems.

These action programmes are a combination of legislative measures and provision of funding for environmental research. Over one hundred legislative measures have been implemented so far, including controls on water pollution, the setting of common standards for factory emissions of sulphur dioxide and the banning of chlorofluorocarbons (CFCs).

Single European Act

These action programmes are not being undertaken in isolation. In 1987, the Community re-affirmed its intention to have a common European market , when all Member States signed the Single European Act. This Act reinforced the commitment of all Member States to policy areas of particular concern, including environmental issues. The Act, summarised in Appendix I on page 59, commits all Member States to respond to deteriorating environmental conditions and states that environmental considerations must be a component of all other Community policy.

Recent policies and programmes

As a result of this increased environmental concern, all projects receiving EC grants and funds are audited for environmental soundness. In addition, standards deemed as essential for health and safety are being harmonised across the Community in the 1992 programme to ensure that all the peoples of Europe are provided with a fundamental level of protection from environmental deterioration.

European Environment Agency

Progress is still being made to tackle the increasing problems that advances in technologies present to the environment. In 1989, the Commission proposed the creation of a European Environment Agency as a scientific and technical centre of excellence to combat pollution. This agency will act as a centre of information, not only for the Community, but also for other interested countries. Research will be undertaken to develop new methods to protect the environment. The agency will be particularly concerned with the quality of the air, waters and soils of Europe as well as their usage.

The Commission recognises that the agency must have the freedom to work at all levels, unfettered by bureaucratic restrictions. It is expected that the agency will not only work with national governments but all manner of international organisations concerned with the environment, such as the United Nations Environmental Programme (UNEP).

Some scepticism has been expressed by Member States as to the necessity of establishing a new body to undertake this type of action.

Within the European Commission, a Directorate General (DG XI) is devoted to environmental issues headed up by Ripa di Meana, the current Commissioner. Generally, Ripa di Meana is considered to be a driving force in developing further measures. However, even within the Commission itself there are conflicting objectives between protecting the environment and other economic priorities.

Legislative measures

GENERAL PROVISIONS AND PROGRAMMES

Regulation (EEC) No 1365/75 of the Council of 26 May 1975 on the creation of a European Foundation for the improvement of living and working conditions.
OJ L 139, 30.05.75, p. 1 *
M by 179H
M by 185I

75/436/Euratom, ECSC, EEC: Council Recommendation of 3 March 1975 regarding cost allocation and action by public authorities on environmental matters.
OJ L 194, 25.07.75, p. 1

Council Resolution of 3 March 1975 on energy and the environment.
OJ C 168, 25.07.75, p. 2

Council Resolution of 24 June 1975 concerning a revised list of second-category pollutants to be studied as part of the programme of action of the European Communities on the environment.
OJ C 168, 25.07.75, p. 4

* **Official Journal of the European Communities (OJ): series agreed (L); series proposed (C); amended by (M); derogated from (D); supplemented by (C); implemented by (O); extended by (E).**

Council Resolution of 15 July 1975 on the adaptation to technical progress of Directives or other Community rules on the protection and improvement of the environment.
OJ C 168, 25.07.75, p. 5
M by 179H

76/161/EEC: Council Decision of 8 December 1975 establishing a common procedure for the setting up and constant updating of an inventory of sources of information on the environment in the Community.
OJ L 031, 05.02.76, p. 8

Resolution of the ECSC Consultative Committee on the Community's Environmental Protection Policies.
OJ C 114, 28.04.84, p. 2

85/338/EEC: Council Decision of 27 June 1985 on the adoption of the Commission work programme concerning an experimental project for gathering, coordinating and ensuring the consistency of information on the state of the environment and natural resources in the Community.
OJ L 176, 06.07.85, p. 14

85/337/EEC: Council Directive of 27 June 1985 on the assessment of the effects of certain public and private projects on the environment.
OJ L 175, 05.07.85, p. 40

86/479/EEC: Commission Decision of 18 September 1986 establishing an Advisory Committee on the protection of the environment in areas under serious threat (Mediterranean basin).
OJ L 282, 03.10.86, p. 23

Council Regulation (EEC) No 2242/87 of 23 July 1987 on action by the Community relating to the environment.
OJ L 207, 29.07.87, p. 8

Council Resolution of 16 December 1986 on the strengthening of Community action in favour of the environment.
OJ C 003, 07.01.87, p. 3

Council Resolution of 3 May 1988 on the close of the European Year of the Environment.
OJ C 129, 18.05.88, p. 1

Agreement of the Representatives of the Governments of the Member States meeting in Council of 5 March 1973 on information for the Commission and for the Member States with a view to possible harmonisation throughout the Communities of urgent measures concerning the protection of the environment.
OJ C 009, 15.03.73, p. 1
O by 474A0720(01) (OJ C 086, 20.07.74, p. 2)

Resolution of the Council and of the representatives of the governments of the Member States of the European Communities, meeting within the Council of 3 October 1984, on the link between the environment and development.
OJ C 272, 12.10.84, p. 1

Resolution of the Council of the European Communities and of the representatives of the governments of the Member States, meeting within the Council of 19 October 1987 on the continuation and implementation of a European Community policy and action programme on the environment (1987–1992).
OJ C 328, 07.12.87, p. 1

3 Water

EC situation

The importance of a policy concerned with the protection of our waterways has been highlighted recently with the disaster in Prince William Sound and the subsequent devastation of a large proportion of Alaska's natural beauty. This incident involved an oil tanker hitting an iceberg and releasing large amounts of crude oil into the sea. However, it is not only accidents that must be guarded against; the intentional dumping of dangerous substances into our waters must also be controlled.

Standards currently in force for drinking and bathing water differ widely between the Member States despite the fact that standards were agreed for bathing water in 1975 and drinking water in 1980. For example, nitrate levels in certain regions of the UK exceed those deemed by the Commission to be acceptable. The question of complying with the EC standards is coming under close scrutiny in the UK at the present time as the government finds itself unable to comply with the deadlines that have been imposed by the Commission. Original deadlines were for 1989, but the UK, unable to meet these, has now agreed a 1995 deadline. This is not acceptable to the Commission, which is taking the UK to court.

Furthermore, the privatisation of the water industry in the UK raises doubts that high standards will be maintained, or whether the necessary investment will be made in the industry post privatisation. The government's multi-million pound advertising campaign attempted to address the British public's concerns.

EC policy

The main thrust of the EC's policy for water is the prevention of the pollution at its source. This policy has the following major strands:

Setting minimum standards

The starting point for the Commission's policy has been the setting of minimum standards for water, depending on its usage. For example, standards have been set for bathing water, drinking water and the waters that support fish life. In addition to the standards themselves, systems have been set up to monitor the Community's water resources and ensure compliance with the standards.

Protection of aquatic life from dangerous substances

In addition to adopting minimum standards, the Commission has put forward many proposals concerning pollution by dangerous substances. A framework Directive was adopted by the Council of Ministers as early as 1976 which was aimed at preventing pollution by particularly toxic products. In more recent years, this has been supplemented by a series of measures.

The most recent action in this area has been the proposal by the Commission, in 1988, aimed at reducing the levels of nitrates that are present in our waters. Primarily aimed at the quality of drinking water, it should also prevent the excessive growth of algae and other aquatic plants that are caused by very high nitrate levels. This measure has a different emphasis than the 1980 Directive on drinking water which set maximum allowable levels of nitrates in drinking water. The proposal aims to reduce the level of nitrates that are input into our waterways through, for example, the reduction in the use of fertilisers spread on agricultural land.

Protection of the sea against oil pollution

Because of the serious consequences of an accidental oil spill, this is considered to be an area of particular importance by the Commission. An Advisory Committee has been set up whose primary task is to co-ordinate national policies and contingency plans in the event of a spill, and to encourage the exchange of information and ideas between the Member States. The Committee's sphere of influence was extended in 1985 to include pollution from other dangerous substances as well as oil.

Of course, a large proportion of sea pollution is not accidental but is the result of the deliberate dumping of waste. The Community is concentrating its efforts on international co-operation in this area and is party to a number of international conventions which provide limitations on the dumping of waste at sea. It is the continuance and expansion of this area that is considered to be an important part of the Community's policy in the future.

Industry specific measures

The Community has targeted specific industries which are the largest contributors to the pollution of our waterways. For example, the titanium dioxide industry has come under particularly close scrutiny.

Conservation

A further element of the Community's policy on water is concerned with the monitoring of our water resources and encouraging the conservation of our supplies.

What remains to be done?

The adoption of measures aimed at combating water pollution must of course continue. However, it appears that the real struggle at the present time is to speed up the implementation process. The recent disagreement between the Commission and the UK is a good illustration of this need. Furthermore, an increased programme of public and corporate education must be embarked upon to discourage wilful acts of pollution. Water pollution stemming from run-off, containing poisonous herbicides and pesticides, must also be addressed.

13

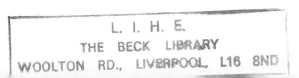

Legislative measures

WATER PROTECTION AND MANAGEMENT

75/440/EEC: Council Directive of 16 June 1975 concerning the quality required of surface water intended for the abstraction of drinking water in the Member States.
OJ L 194, 25.07.75, p. 26
M by 379L0869 (OJ L 271, 29.10.79, p. 44)

76/160/EEC: Council Directive of 8 December 1975 concerning the quality of bathing water.
OJ L 031, 05.02.76, p. 1
M by 179H
M by 185I

76/464/EEC: Council Directive of 4 May 1976 on pollution caused by certain dangerous substances discharged into the aquatic environment of the Community.
OJ L 129, 18.05.76, p. 23

POLLUTION AND NUISANCES

77/795/EEC: Council Decision of 12 December 1977 establishing a common procedure for the exchange of information on the quality of surface fresh water in the Community.
OJ L 334, 24.12.77, p. 29
M by 179H
M by 185I
C by 381D0856 (OJ L 319, 07.11.81, p. 17)
M by 384D0422 (OJ L 237, 05.09.84, p. 15)
M by 386D0574 (OJ L 335, 28.11.86, p. 44)

Council Resolution of 26 June 1978 setting up an action programme of the European Communities on the control and reduction of pollution caused by hydrocarbons discharged at sea.
OJ C 162, 08.07.78, p. 1

79/869/EEC: Council Directive of 9 October 1979 concerning

the methods of measurement and frequencies of sampling and analysis of surface water intended for the abstraction of drinking water in the Member States.
OJ L 271, 29.10.79, p. 44
M by 185I
M by 381L0855 (OJ L 319, 07.11.81, p. 16)

79/923/EEC: Council Directive of 30 October 1979 on the quality required of shellfish waters.
OJ L 281, 10.11.79, p. 47

80/686/EEC: Commission Decision of 25 June 1980 setting up an Advisory Committee on the control and reduction of pollution caused by hydrocarbons discharged at sea.
OJ L 188, 22.07.80, p. 11
M by 385D0208 (OJ L 089, 29.03.85, p. 64)
M by 387D0144 (OJ L 057, 27.02.87, p. 57)

80/68/EEC: Council Directive of 17 December 1979 on the protection of groundwater against pollution caused by certain dangerous substances.
OJ L 020, 26.01.80, p. 43

80/778/EEC: Council Directive of 15 July 1980 relating to the quality of water intended for human consumption.
OJ L 229, 30.08.80, p. 11
M by 185I
M by 381L0858 (OJ L 319, 07.11.81, p. 19)

82/176/EEC: Council Directive of 22 March 1982 on limit values and quality objectives for mercury discharges by the chlor-alkali electrolysis industry.
OJ L 081, 27.03.82, p. 29

83/513/EEC: Council Directive of 26 September 1983 on limit values and quality objectives for cadmium discharges.
OJ L 291, 24.10.83, p. 1

Council Resolution of 7 February 1983 concerning the combating of water pollution.
OJ C 046, 17.02.83, p. 17

84/491/EEC: Council Directive of 9 October 1984 on limit values and quality objectives for discharges of hexachloro-cyclohexane.
OJ L 274, 17.10.84, p. 11

86/85/EEC: Council Decision of 6 March 1986 establishing a Community information system for the control and reduction of pollution caused by the spillage of hydrocarbons and other harmful substances at sea.
OJ L 077, 22.03.86, p. 33
M by 388D0346 (OJ L 158, 25.06.88, p. 32)

Water protection and management

86/280/EEC: Council Directive of 12 June 1986 on limit values and quality objectives for discharges of certain dangerous substances included in List I of the Annex to Directive 76/464/EEC.
OJ L 181, 04.07.86, p. 16
M by 388L0347 (OJ L 158, 25.06.88, p. 35)

Resolution of the Council and of the representatives of the governments of the Member States of the European Communities, meeting within the Council of 3 October 1984, on new forms of cooperation in the sphere of water.
OJ C 272, 12.10.84, p. 2

78/659/EEC: Council Directive of 18 July 1978 on the quality of fresh waters needing protection or improvement in order to support fish life.
OJ L 222, 14.08.78, p. 1
M by 179H
M by 185I

82/883/EEC: Council Directive of 3 December 1982 on procedures for the surveillance and monitoring of environments concerned by waste from the titanium dioxide industry.
OJ L 378, 31.12.82, p. 1
M by 185I

4 Air

EC situation

Pollutants in the atmosphere, such as sulphur dioxide, fall back to earth as acid deposits contaminating crops, damaging forests and killing living organisms in lakes and rivers. Airborne pollutants also corrode metal structures and paintwork.

The major causes of this damage to forests, lakes, crops and buildings in the Community can be attributed to the combustion of fossil fuels by:

- power plants
- motor vehicles
- central heating plants.

The Commission has estimated that the cost to the Community of this type of atmospheric pollution may be as high as £60 million every year.

EC policy

Vehicle emissions

In the 1970s, before the Community had implemented a coherent environmental policy, it was tabling legislation to curb air pollution. Motor vehicle exhaust fumes were the focus of Commission attention to ensure that noxious emissions were progressively reduced. Thus, a series of directives to limit the sulphur content of certain fuels and the lead and benzene content of petrol addressed:

- petrol powered motor vehicles

- diesel powered motor vehicles
- agricultural tractors.

More recently (in March 1985) a directive was adopted which required the general introduction of lead-free petrol across the Community by, at the latest, October 1989. In addition, requirements for stricter emission standards were laid down for all cars manufactured in the Community as of October 1988. The introduction of lead-free petrol is the first stage in reducing motoring pollution. Cars are increasingly being fitted with catalytic converters as a standard or optional feature. For example, Audi has announced that it will fit catalytic converters to all its UK-sold cars for the 1990s.

Catalytic converters can reduce the emissions of nitrous oxide, hydrocarbons and carbon monoxide by up to 90 per cent. However, although this reduces the causes of acid rain and respiratory diseases, a catalytic converter does emit three times more carbon dioxide, the major 'greenhouse gas'.

Air quality standards

An important aspect of air pollution policy relates to the setting of air quality standards to which all Member states must adhere. The standards cover the following pollutants which cause acid rain and various respiratory diseases:

- sulphur dioxide
- suspended particulate matter (SPM)
- lead dioxide; and
- nitrogen dioxide.

Progress has been made in setting standards for most of these pollutants. In 1980, legislation was adopted establishing limits for sulphur dioxide and SPM. Two years later, guidelines were developed on the acceptable level of lead in ambient air. A third directive, adopted in March 1985, established air quality standards for nitrogen dioxide.

Member States' implementation of these directives should alter the level of air pollution in the Community. In order to adhere to the specific limits set by the legislation, Member States will have to reduce progressively:

- the amounts of sulphur dioxide and SPM being discharged into the atmosphere, particularly by industry
- the level of lead emissions produced by petrol fuelled engines
- nitrogen dioxide emanating from traffic, industrial plants and heavy diesel engines.

Industrial plants

Given the significant air pollution that is caused by industrial plants, a directive was adopted in 1984 which establishes an important principle: industrial operators should use the best available technology (which does not entail excessive costs) for major new industrial developments. This principle will gradually be extended to existing industrial premises and, eventually, to the introduction of an EC-wide emission standard for 'stationary industrial sources of air pollution'.

Monitoring

Clearly, these directives are an important step in the right direction. However, to assist in monitoring their effectiveness, a system was established in 1985 to undertake the biological screening of Community citizens to monitor body lead levels.

Each Member State must designate a competent national authority to undertake the screenings, fifty of which need to be undertaken per million inhabitants. The screenings will rely on volunteers.

More recently, a common procedure has been established to exchange the results of national monitoring of sulphur dioxide, SPM, carbon dioxide, nitrogen dioxide, heavy metals and ozone measured in the atmosphere.

Energy policy

Energy policy is inextricably linked with air pollution policy due to energy production's dependence on fossil fuels. Environmental considerations, such as minimising emissions, inevitably affect the costs of producing alternative types of energy. Actions taken in the pursuit of economic policy objectives must also be seen in the light of their environmental effects. Improving the quality of air is being sought through:

- minimising emissions from fossil fuel power stations
- energy conservation measures
- development of alternatives to fossil fuels.

However, short-term commercial objectives are clearly a major obstacle to environmentally sound practices.

What remains to be done?

Despite the adoption of directives on the discharge of sulphur dioxide, the use of CFCs in aerosol cans and the control of pollution from certain industrial premises, progress has been slow in two key areas:

- pollution from large combustion plants
- emission of gases from motor vehicles.

Both of these have detrimental effects on forests through acid rain and on public health. Member States were not in agreement on Commission proposals in these two areas. Lack of consensus was based on the definition of acceptable standards and on a timetable for implementing restrictive measures. Due to the need for harmonised standards across the Community, countries such as Holland, which provided tax incentives to consumers purchasing cars with environmentally friendly catalytic converters, were in fact reprimanded by the Commission and the practice outlawed.

However, the 1987 Single European Act, enabling majority rather than unanimous voting for this type of legislation, has resulted in accelerated progress. For example, a series of car vehicle emissions have now been adopted. Still to be established are standards for air pollution from major industrial plants not covered by existing directives (such as nuclear installations and plants burning fuel oil and solid fuels).

Proposals are also due in the following areas:

- reducing air pollution from means of transport not already addressed by legislation
- establishing air quality standards for certain pollutants such as photochemicals oxidants.

Future policies

By 1987, the Commission was developing a longer-term strategy to reduce air pollution both within the EC and at a global level. The major objectives of this strategy are to:

- identify major indoor and outdoor air pollutants which are at the moment, or may be in the future, detrimental to public health and the environment
- set EC-wide goals in order to reduce significantly the total emissions of pollution from all sources into the air. In addition, to establish procedures to ensure that these goals are being met
- to reduce ambient air concentrations of the most important pollutants to a level which is deemed acceptable for the most sensitive ecosystems.

Legislative measures

SPACE, ENVIRONMENT AND NATURAL RESOURCES

Council Regulation (EEC) No 3528/86 of 17 November 1986 on the protection of the Community's forests against atmospheric pollution.
OJ L 326, 21.11.86, p. 2
O by 387R0526 (OJ L 053, 21.02.87, p. 14)

Commission Regulation (EEC) No 526/87 of 20 February 1987 laying down certain detailed rules for the application of Council Regulation (EEC) No 3528/86 on the protection of the Community's forests against atmospheric pollution.
OJ L 053, 21.02.87, p. 14

Commission Regulation (EEC) No 1696/87 of 10 June 1987 laying down certain detailed rules for the implementation of Council Regulation (EEC) No 3528/86 on the protection of the Community's forests against atmospheric pollution (inventories, network, reports).
OJ L 161, 22.06.87, p. 1

Commission Regulation (EEC) No 1697/87 of 10 June 1987 laying down certain detailed rules for the implementation of Council Regulation (EEC) No 3528/86 on the protection of the Community's forests against atmospheric pollution (payment of aid).
OJ L 161, 22.06.87, p. 23

MONITORING OF ATMOSPHERIC POLLUTION

70/220/EEC: Council Directive of 20 March 1970 on the approximation of the laws of the Member States relating to measures to be taken against air pollution by gases from positive-ignition engines of motor vehicles.
OJ L 076, 06.04.70, p. 1
E by 172B
M by 374L0290 (OJ L 159, 15.06.74, p. 61)
E by 377L0102 (OJ L 032, 03.02.77, p. 32)
M by 378L0665 (OJ L 223, 14.08.78, p. 48)
M by 383L0351 (OJ L 197, 20.07.83, p. 1)
M by 388L0076 (OJ L 036, 09.02.88, p. 1)
M by 388L0436 (OJ L 214, 06.08.88, p. 1)

72/306/EEC: Council Directive of 2 August 1972 on the approximation of the laws of the Member States relating to the measures to be taken against the emission of pollutants from

diesel engines for use in vehicles.
OJ L 190, 20.08.72, p. 1

75/716/EEC: Council Directive of 24 November 1975 on the approximation of the laws of the Member States relating to the sulphur content of certain liquid fuels.
OJ L 307, 27.11.75, p. 22
M by 387L0219 (OJ L 091, 03.04.87, p. 19)

79/872/EEC: Commission Decision of 10 October 1979 concerning the notification by the Luxembourg Government of a derogation from Directive 75/716/EEC pursuant to Article 2 (3) of the Directive.
OJ L 269, 26.10.79, p. 28

77/537/EEC: Council Directive of 28 June 1977 on the approximation of the laws of the Member states relating to the measures to be taken against the emission of pollutants from diesel engines for use in wheeled agricultural or forestry tractors.
OJ L 220, 29.08.77, p. 38
M by 382L0890 (OJ L 378, 31.12.82, p. 45)

80/779/EEC: Council Directive of 15 July 1980 on air quality limit values and guide values for sulphur dioxide and suspended particulates.
OJ L 229, 30.08.80, p. 30
M by 185I
M by 381L0857 (OJ L 319, 07.11.81, p. 18)

Council Resolution of 15 July 1980 on transboundary air pollution by sulphur dioxide and suspended particulates.
OJ C 222, 30.08.80, p. 1

82/459/EEC: Council Decision of 24 June 1982 establishing a reciprocal exchange of information and data from networks and individual stations measuring air pollution within the Member States.
OJ L 210, 19.07.82, p. 1

POLLUTION AND NUISANCES
MONITORING AND ATMOSPHERIC POLLUTION

82/884/EEC: Council Directive of 3 December 1982 on a limit value for lead in the air.
OJ L 378, 31.12.82, p. 15

84/360/EEC: Council Directive of 28 June 1984 on the combating of air pollution from industrial plants.
OJ L 188, 16.07.84, p. 20

85/203/EEC: Council Directive of 7 March 1985 on air quality standards for nitrogen dioxide.
OJ L 087, 27.03.85, p. 1
M by 385L0580 (OJ L 372, 31.12.85, p. 36)

85/210/EEC: Council Directive of 20 March 1985 on the approximation of the laws of the Member States concerning the lead content of petrol.
OJ L 096, 03.04.85, p. 25
M by 385L0581 (OJ L 372, 31.12.85, p. 37)
M by 387L0416 (OJ L 225, 13.08.87, p. 33)

87/217/EEC: Council Directive of 19 March 1987 on the prevention and reduction of environmental pollution by asbestos.
OJ L 085, 28.03.87, p. 40

88/77/EEC: Council Directive of 3 December 1987 on the approximation of the laws of the Member States relating to the measures to be taken against the emission of gaseous pollutants from diesel engines for use in vehicles.
OJ L 036, 09.02.88, p. 33

88/609/EEC: Council Directive of 24 November 1988 on the limitation of emissions of certain pollutants into the air from large combustion plants.
OJ L 336, 07.12.88, p. 1

Council Regulation (EEC) No 3322/88 of 14 October 1988 on certain chlorofluorocarbons and halons which deplete the ozone layer.
OJ L 297, 31.10.88, p. 1

Council Resolution of 14 October 1988 for the limitation of use of chlorofluorocarbons and halons.
OJ C 285, 09.11.88, p. 1

89/349/EEC: Commission Recommendation of 13 April 1989 on the reduction of chlorofluorocarbons by the aerosol industry.
OJ L 144, 27.05.89, p. 56

PREVENTION OF NOISE POLLUTION

70/157/EEC: Council Directive of 6 February 1970 on the approximation of the laws of the Member States relating to the permissible sound level and the exhaust system of motor vehicles.
OJ L 042, 23.02.70, p. 16
M by 172B
M by 185I
M by 373L0350 (OJ L 321, 22.11.73, p. 33)
M by 377L0212 (OJ L 066, 12.03.77, p. 33)
M by 381L0334 (OJ L 131, 18.05.81, p. 6)
M by 384L0372 (OJ L 196, 26.07.84, p. 47)
M by 384L0424 (OJ L 238, 06.09.84, p. 31)
M by 387L0354 (OJ L 192, 11.07.87, p. 43)

78/1015/EEC: Council Directive of 23 November 1978 on the approximation of the laws of the Member States on the permissible sound level and exhaust system of motorcycles.
OJ L 349, 13.12.78, p. 21
M by 179H
C by 185I
M by 387L0056 (OJ L 024, 27.01.87, p. 42)
M by 389L0235 (OJ L 098, 11.04.89, p. 1)

5 Waste Management

EC situation

Every year, Europeans generate in excess of 2000 million tonnes of waste – both domestic and industrial. Industrial waste forms around 10 per cent of this and highly toxic substances a further 2 per cent. Table 1 on page 27 shows the various sources of domestic waste.

It is this smallest proportion of toxic waste that poses the largest threat to the environment and presents the biggest problem to the Community. Facilities for the safe disposal of toxic waste are hopelessly inadequate, and as the available facilities are exhausted the sea becomes increasingly used as a dumping ground. However, industry is responding to the general concern for the environment. For example, ICI has recently announced that it will stop dumping chemical waste in the North Sea in the early 1990s. The intervening period is required to investigate alternative methods of disposal.

Although the majority of domestic waste is relatively harmless as compared with some toxic chemicals, it still does pose a large problem of disposal. The use of landfill sites, a common method of disposal, is being questioned for health and safety reasons. An incident occurred in the UK in 1988 where a house near a landfill site was completely destroyed by an explosion caused by the build-up of methane gas coming from the landfill, although it had been sealed for many years. In the UK, the problem is compounded by the large amounts of waste that are imported to be processed and disposed of; even as our own facilities can scarcely cope with our own domestic waste. The UK government recently launched a campaign for greater recycling of waste as an alternative to landfill dumping.

However, as individuals become increasingly environmentally conscious, steps are being made to reduce household waste. For example, 'bottle banks' are an increasingly common sight and the use of recycled paper is expanding rapidly. West Germany, Holland and Belgium are far ahead of the UK in using these recycling measures. See Table 2 below.

Table 1: European Domestic Waste (1986)

Kitchen waste	30%
Paper	25%
Dust/ashes	10%
Glass	10%
Textiles	10%
Metal	8%
Plastics	7%

Source: Friends of the Earth

Table 2: European Glass Recycling

Percentage share national consumption retrieved

Switzerland	55%
Netherlands	53%
Belgium	50%
Italy	40%
West Germany	39%
France	34%
Denmark	27%
Spain	23%
Greece	16%
UK	15%
Portugal	13%
Eire	10%

Source: Glass Gazette

EC policy

The EC's policy towards waste management has three main objectives. These are:

- to recycle and re-use waste to the maximum possible extent
- to reduce the quantity of unrecoverable waste
- to dispose of as safely as possible any unrecoverable waste.

Several measures have been adopted to satisfy these objectives:

- as early as 1975 a directive concerning waste generally was adopted by the Council of Ministers. It required Member States to take action by drawing up plans for environmentally sound methods of waste disposal and to encourage all types of waste recovery and recycling
- in 1978, the framework directive controlling the disposal of toxic substances was adopted. This directive contained a list of dangerous and toxic substances and laid down rules governing labelling, storage, treatment, disposal and transport. It also set out provisions prohibiting uncontrolled dumping and tipping. The list of dangerous substances has been supplemented by further directives in recent years
- a recent proposal from the Commission concerns the regulation of emissions which arise as a result of the incineration of municipal waste
- the Commission is carrying out a series of measures which are aimed at reducing the amount of waste that is generated. Their efforts are concentrated on the development of low polluting and low waste-producing 'clean technologies'. Areas covered include the paper industry, the textile industry, mining and quarrying and the agri-food industry.

An issue that has recently been discussed in the context of waste-management policy and its conflict with other Community policies is the restrictions on the sale of non-alcoholic drinks in Denmark. The Danes insist that drinks may only be sold in returnable bottles (with environmental considerations in mind) which effectively excludes any foreign competition from the market. Although it is appropriate in the eyes of the environmentalists, it goes against the principle of free competition. However, the European Court ruled that environmental considerations, in this case, ride above free competition.

It may be that recycling of waste is not always compatible with other elements of EC environmental policy. For example, the spreading of manure on agricultural land could be seen to be an effective reclamation policy. However, the Commission's policy for water protection requires that manure spreading be limited to ensure the quality of water supplies.

What remains to be done?

As landfill sites rapidly become full and as our lifestyle becomes increasingly 'disposable', new solutions have to be found to manage our waste. Not only must the Commission lay down new measures, but sources of finance for their implementation must also be agreed.

Legislative measures

NUCLEAR SAFETY AND RADIOACTIVE WASTE

75/406/Euratom: Council Decision of 26 June 1975 adopting a programme on the management and storage of radioactive waste.
OJ L 178, 09.07.75, p. 28

Council Resolution of 26 June 1975 extending the powers of the Advisory Committee on Programme Management for 'Treatment and storage of radioactive waste' (direct action) and 'Management and storage of radioactive waste' (indirect action).
OJ C 153, 09.07.75, p. 10

Council Resolution of 18 February 1980 concerning the Advisory Committee on Programme Management for the management and storage of radioactive waste.
OJ C 051, 29.02.80, p. 4

Council Resolution of 18 February 1980 on the implementa-

---

tion of a Community plan of action in the field of radioactive waste.
OJ C 051, 29.02.80, p. 1

POLLUTION AND NUISANCES

CouncilResolution of 18 February 1980 on the reprocessing of irradiated nuclear fuels.
OJ C 051, 29.02.80, p. 4

82/74/Euratom: Commission Recommendation of 3 February 1982 on the storage and reprocessing of irradiated nuclear fuels.
OJ L 037, 10.02.82, p. 36

85/199/Euratom: Council Decision of 12 March 1985 adopting a research and development programme on the management and storage of radioactive waste (1985 to 1989).
OJ L 083, 25.03.85, p. 20

WASTE MANAGEMENT AND CLEAN TECHNOLOGY

75/439/EEC: Council Directive of 16 June 1975 on the disposal of waste oils.
OJ L 194, 25.07.75, p. 23
M by 387L0101 (OJ L 042, 12.02.87, p. 43)

75/442/EEC: Council Directive of 15 July 1975 on waste.
OJ L 194, 25.07.75, p. 39

76/431/EEC: Commission Decision of 21 April 1976 setting up a Committee on Waste Management.
OJ L 115, 01.05.76, p. 73
M by 179H
M by 185I

76/403/EEC: Council Directive of 6 April 1976 on the disposal of polychlorinated biphenyls and polychlorinated terphenyls.
OJ L 108, 26.04.76, p. 41

78/176/EEC: Council Directive of 20 February 1978 on waste from the titanium dioxide industry.

OJ L 054, 25.02.78, p. 19
M by 382L0883 (OJ L 378, 31.12.82, p. 1)
M by 383L0029 (OJ L 032, 03.02.83, p. 28)

78/319/EEC: Council Directive of 20 March 1978 on toxic and dangerous waste.
OJ L 084, 31.03.78, p. 43
M by 179H
M by 185I

82/883/EEC: Council Directive of 3 December 1982 on procedures for the surveillance and monitoring of environments concerned by waste from the titanium dioxide industry.
OJ L 378, 31.12.82, p. 1
M by 185I

SPACE, ENVIRONMENT AND NATURAL RESOURCES

WASTE MANAGEMENT AND CLEAN TECHNOLOGY

81/972/EEC: Council Recommendation of 3 December 1981 concerning the re-use of waste paper and the use of recycled paper.
OJ L 355, 10.12.81, p. 56

84/631/EEC: Council Directive of 6 December 1984 on the supervision and control within the European Community of the transfrontier shipment of hazardous waste.
OJ L 326, 13.12.84, p. 31
M by 385L0469 (OJ L 272, 12.10.85, p. 1)
M by 386L0121 (OJ L 100, 16.04.86, p. 20)
M by 386L0279 (OJ L 181, 04.07.86, p. 13)

85/339/EEC: Council Directive of 27 June 1985 on containers of liquids for human consumption.
OJ L 176, 06.07.85, p. 18

86/278/EEC: Council Directive of 12 June 1986 on the protection of the environment, and in particular of the soil, when sewage sludge is used in agriculture.
OJ L 181, 04.07.86, p. 6

6 Chemicals

EC situation

In the area of chemical pollution, incidents such as the 1983 Seveso spillage of a shipment of dioxin and the 1984 Bhopal release of poisonous gas have altered Community policy. As a result of this the emphasis has shifted away from developing legislation specific to particular chemical substances towards developing an overall approach in minimising environmental risks associated with all potentially harmful chemicals.

EC policy

A new approach

What is now known as the first generation of Community environmental legislation focused on controlling specific substances. For example, a directive was adopted in 1973 regarding the composition of detergents.

However, the Commission soon recognised that few of the 120 000 chemicals available in the EC had undergone any form of testing for their risks to human health or the potential impact on the environment. Clearly, a new approach was required given that:

- testing all chemical substances already available is not feasible as it would literally take centuries
- every year, between 100 and 200 new chemicals appear on the market.

The approach required is one of prevention, through the anticipation and control of risks and hazards not only by legislative bodies but also by industry and the public.

Notification system

As long ago as 1976, legislation had been developed for the classification, packaging and labelling of dangerous substances. Under the new approach, in 1979, this directive was further amended to establish an EC-wide notification system for new chemicals. This new system is based on the manufacturer or importer submitting (to one Member State) a base set of data and a risk assessment. This base set of data for a new chemical includes information concerning its:

- physico-chemical characteristics
- potential health and environmental effects
- uses
- quantities produced
- proposed classification and labelling; and
- an overall assessment of its risks.

The Commission and individual Member States may request, given certain conditions and production levels, further detailed information concerning a chemical substance.

This new system has created a 12-country system of interlocking procedures and obligations in which every Member State acts as the agent of other Member States by admitting a new chemical into the whole of the Community.

Not only is the base set of information passed to other Member States and to the Commission itself but it is also made available to the public.

This directive has two advantages:

- for national bodies and the consumer, it provides comprehensive information detailing uses and risks of new chemicals which is systematically updated
- for the manufacturer, it avoids duplication in notification procedures. A chemical registered in one Member State may be freely sold across the Community. This is much simpler than, for example, the multiple applications currently required for the marketing of pharmaceuticals in the EC.

Emergency response planning

In the aftermath of the Seveso incident in 1982, a further directive was adopted, commonly known as the 'Seveso Directive'. In essence, this laid down emergency response planning procedures and included these requirements following significant industrial accidents:

- a comprehensive notification system
- the obligation to inform and consult the public in developing emergency plans
- the same obligation towards bordering Member States.

The Seveso Directive has since been used as a model across the world. In particular, it was used following the release of harmful gas in an industrial plant in Bhopal. More recently, the directive was used as a basis for emergency response planning for nuclear installations, following the Chernobyl disaster in 1987.

Given the importance of these directives, the Commission took the unusual step of closely monitoring Member State implementation. On a regular basis, national authorities were called to Brussels to compare progress, share specific experience and jointly to formulate pragmatic procedures and standards.

Dealing with existing chemicals

But what of the chemicals that were already on the market in 1979, before this new approach was adopted by the Commission? A new approach is being developed in this area too. Information is being gathered about a small group of these chemicals, those that are known to be dangerous. Ultimately, it may be that the legislative emphasis on the marketing and use of dangerous chemicals will be broadened to include comprehensive testing, evaluation and control procedures.

Further policies

New policies are also progressing in other areas:

- combining existing legislation on cadmium, asbestos and lead to improve monitoring and control of their effects on the environment
- continuing close co-operation with the OECD to implement existing and new international agreements
- participating in other international agreements, such as the Geneva Convention in the case of chlorofluorocarbons to protect the ozone layer.

The European Parliament in particular is lobbying for increasingly stringent controls on chemicals, given the tragic consequences of incidents such as Bhopal and the potential impact of future chemical accidents.

Legislative measures

NUCLEAR SAFETY AND RADIOACTIVE WASTE

EAEC Council: Directives laying down the basic standards for the protection of the health of workers and the general public against the dangers arising from ionizing radiations.
OJ L 011, 20.02.59, p. 221
M by 362L1633 (OJ L 057, 09.07.62, p. 1633)

76/579/Euratom: Council Directive of 1 June 1976 laying down the revised basic safety standards for the health protection of the general public and workers against the dangers of ionizing radiation.
OJ L 187, 12.07.76, p. 1
M by 379L0343 (OJ L 083, 03.04.79, p. 18)
D by 380L0836 (OJ L 246, 17.09.80, p. 1)

80/237/Euratom: Council Decision of 18 February 1980 on the setting up of an 'ad hoc' Advisory Committee on the Reprocessing of Irradiated Nuclear Fuels.
OJ L 052, 26.02.80, p. 9

80/836/Euratom: Council Directive of 15 July 1980 amending the Directives laying down the basic safety standards for the health protection of the general public and workers against the dangers of ionizing radiation.
OJ L 246, 17.09.80, p. 1
M by 384L0467 (OJ L 265, 05.10.84, p. 4)

POLLUTION AND NUISANCES

87/600/Euratom: Council Decision of 14 December 1987 on Community arrangements for the early exchange of information in the event of a radiological emergency.
OJ L 371, 30.12.87, p. 76

CHEMICALS, INDUSTRIAL RISK AND BIOTECHNOLOGY

67/548/EEC: Council Directive of 27 June 1967 on the approximation of laws, regulations and administrative provisions relating to the classification, packaging and labelling of dangerous substances.
OJ 196, 16.08.67, p. 1
E by 172B
(amended 19 times, most recently by 388L0490 OJ L 259, 19.09.88, p. 1)

73/404/EEC: Council Directive of 22 November 1973 on the approximation of the laws of the Member States relating to detergents.
OJ L 347, 17.12.73, p. 51
C by 382L0242 (OJ L 109, 22.04.82, p. 1)
M by 386L0094 (OJ L 080, 25.03.86, p. 51)

73/405/EEC: Council Directive of 22 November 1973 on the approximation of the laws of the Member States relating to

methods of testing the biodegradability of anionic surfactants.
OJ L 347, 17.12.73, p. 53
M by 382L0243 (OJ L 109, 22.04.82, p. 18)

76/769/EEC: Council Directive of 27 July 1976 on the approximation of the laws, regulations and administrative provisions of the Member States relating to restrictions on the marketing and use of certain dangerous substances and preparations.
OJ L 262, 27.09.76, p. 201
M by 379L0663 (OJ L 197, 03.08.79, p. 37)
C by 382L0806 (OJ L 339, 01.12.82, p. 55)
C by 382L0828 (OJ L 350, 10.12.82, p. 34)
M by 383L0264 (OJ L 147, 06.06.83, p. 9)
M by 383L0478 (OJ L 263, 24.09.83, p. 33)
M by 385L0467 (OJ L 269, 11.10.85, p. 56)
M by 385L0610 (OJ L 375, 31.12.85, p. 1)

78/618/EEC: Commission Decision of 28 June 1978 setting up a Scientific Advisory Committee to examine the toxicity and ecotoxicity of chemical compounds.
OJ L 198, 22.07.78, p. 17
M by 179H
M by 185I
M by 380D1084 (OJ L 316, 25.11.80, p. 21)
M by 388D0241 (OJ L 105, 26.04.88, p. 29)

Council Resolution of 30 May 1978 on fluorocarbons in the environment.
OJ C 133, 07.06.78, p. 1

79/3/EEC: Council Recommendation of 19 December 1978 to the Member States regarding methods of evaluating the cost of pollution control to industry.
OJ L 005, 09.01.79, p. 28

80/372/EEC: Council Decision of 26 March 1980 concerning chlorofluorocarbons in the environment.
OJ L 090, 03.04.80, p. 45

81/437/EEC: Commission Decision of 11 May 1981 laying

down the criteria in accordance with which information relating to the inventory of chemical substances is supplied by the Member States to the Commission.
OJ L 167, 24.06.81, p. 31

82/795/EEC: Council Decision of 15 November 1982 on the consolidation of precautionary measures concerning chlorofluorocarbons in the environment.
OJ L 329, 25.11.82, p. 29

82/501/EEC: Council Directive of 24 June 1982 on the major-accident hazards of certain industrial activities.
OJ L 230, 05.08.82, p. 1
M by 185I
M by 387L0216 (OJ L 085, 28.03.87, p. 36)
M by 388L0610 (OJ L 336, 07.12.88, p. 14)

84/156/EEC: Council Directive of 8 March 1984 on limit values and quality objectives for mercury discharges by sectors other than the chlor-alkali electrolysis industry.
OJ L 074, 17.03.84, p. 49

85/71/EEC: Commission Decision of 21 December 1984 concerning the list of chemical substances notified pursuant to Council Directive 67/548/EEC on the approximation of laws, regulations and administrative provisions relating to the classification, packaging and labelling of dangerous substances.
OJ L 030, 02.02.85, p. 33

87/18/EEC: Council Directive of 18 December 1986 on the harmonisation of laws, regulations and administrative provisions relating to the application of the principles of good laboratory practice and the verification of their applications for tests on chemical substances.
OJ L 015, 17.01.87, p. 29

88/320/EEC: Council Directive of 9 June 1988 on the inspection and verification of Good Laboratory Practice (GLP).
OJ L 145, 11.06.88, p. 35

Council Regulation (EEC) No 1734/88 of 16 June 1988 con-

cerning export from, and import into, the Community of certain dangerous chemicals.
OJ L 155, 22.06.88, p. 2

Council Resolution of 25 January 1988 on a Community action programme to combat environmental pollution by cadmium.
OJ C 030, 04.02.88, p. 1

Council Regulation (EEC) No 428/89 of 20 February 1989 concerning the export of certain chemical products.
OJ L 050, 22.02.89 p. 1

7 Noise

EC situation

The Community suffers in various ways through noise pollution:

- the health and safety of Community citizens is at risk to varying degrees across the Community
- noise has an adverse effect on the environment.

In addition, due to the varying technical noise standards across the Community, there are barriers to trade in goods such as electrical appliances. Some environmental concerns have therefore been addressed in the 1992 legislative programme to complete the Single Market.

EC policy

The Commission has developed a series of directives designed to reduce noise levels. For example, by the 4th December 1989, EC Member States will have implemented a directive concerning noise of household appliances such as washing machines, vacuum cleaners and food processors. This particular directive aims to:

- ensure that the public are given as much information as possible on the noise levels of appliances that they purchase
- help the free movement of household appliances throughout the Community.

All the directives in this series require manufacturers to provide information regarding the noise level of their product to help the user and to facilitate official testing.

So far, the following have been addressed by these directives:

- cars
- buses
- heavy trucks
- sub-sonic aircraft
- lawnmowers
- household appliances.

Construction equipment such as air compressors and pneumatic drills also now have an EC wide noise measurement procedure.

A further area where the Commission is trying to make national EC noise standards compatible relates to the noise emanating from airports, based both on existing and future levels of traffic.

What remains to be done?

Given the growing public concern on noise levels the Commission may accelerate its environmental programme in this area. Under consideration are the following actions:

- defining quality guidelines for noise levels, to be used across the Community
- further product-related noise directives – particularly for vehicles such as motorcycles. The Commission is also considering the inclusion of noise tests for MOT tests across the Community
- to minimise aircraft noise, the Commission is debating whether to apply the 'polluter pays' principle and develop noise-related landing charges.

The general principle as regard to noise is to establish acceptable levels by product and to guide Member States actively to discourage noisy products through national policies.

Legislative measures

POLLUTION AND NUISANCES

PREVENTION OF NOISE POLLUTION

78/1015/EEC: Council Directive of 23 November 1978 on the approximation of the laws of the Member States on the permissible sound level and exhaust system of motorcycles.
OJ L 349, 13.12.78, p. 21
M by 179H
C by 185I
M by 387L0056 (OJ L 024, 27.01.87, p. 42)
M by 389L0235 (OJ L 098, 11.04.89. p. 1)

79/113/EEC: Council Directive of 19 December 1978 on the approximation of the laws of the Member States relating to the determination of the noise emission of construction plant and equipment.
OJ L (33, 08.02.79, p. 15
M by 179H
M by 185I
M by 381L1051 (OJ L 376, 30.12.81, p. 49)
M by 385L0405 (OJ L 233, 30.08.85, p. 9)

80/51/EEC: Council Directive of 20 December 1979 on the limitation of noise emissions from subsonic aircraft.
OJ L 018, 24.01.80, p. 26
M by 383L0206 (OJ L 117, 04.05.83, p. 15)

84/533/EEC: Council Directive of 17 September 1984 on the approximation of the laws of the Member States relating to the permissible sound power level of compressors.
OJ L 300, 19.11.84, p. 123
M by 385L0406 (OJ L 233, 30.08.85, p. 11)

84/534/EEC: Council Directive of 17 September 1984 on the approximation of the laws of the Member States relating to the permissible sound power level of tower cranes.

OJ L 300, 19.11.84, p. 130
M by 387L0405 (OJ L 220, 08.08.87, p. 60)

84/535/EEC: Council Directive of 17 September 1984 on the approximation of the laws of the Member States relating to the permissible sound power level of welding generators.
OJ L 300, 19.11.84, p. 142
M by 385L0407 (OJ L 233, 30.08.85, p. 16)

84/536/EEC: Council Directive of 17 September 1984 on the approximation of the laws of the Member States relating to the permissible sound power level of power generators.
OJ L 300, 19.11.84, p. 149
M by 385L0408 (OJ L 233, 30.08.85, p. 18)

84/537/EEC: Council Directive of 17 September 1984 on the approximation of the laws of the Member States relating to the permissible sound power level of powered hand-held con-crete-breakers and picks.
OJ L 300, 19.11.84, p. 156
M by 385L0409 (OJ L 233, 30.08.85, p. 20)

84/538/EEC: Council Directive of 17 September 1984 on the approximation of the laws of the Member States relating to the permissible sound power level of lawnmowers.
OJ L 300, 19.11.84, p. 171
M by 387L0252 (OJ L 117, 05.05.87, p. 22)
M by 388L0180 (OJ L 081, 26.03.88, p. 69)
M by 388L0181 (OJ L 081, 26.03.88, p. 71)

86/594/EEC: Council Directive of 1 December 1986 on air-borne noise emitted by household appliances.
OJ L 344, 06.12.86, p. 24

86/662/EEC: Council Directive of 22 December 1986 on the limitation of noise emitted by hydraulic excavators, rope-oper-ated excavators, dozers, loaders and excavator-loaders.
OJ L 384, 31.12.86, p. 1

8 Research and Development

The Community has had a programme for research and development in connection with environmental issues since 1973. Its main objective has been to provide a scientific basis for the different elements of the Community's environmental policy and at the same time aid the implementation process by providing a better understanding of the environment.

The programme is split into three areas: contract research, direct action and concerted action.

Contract research

In the contract research programme, contracts are awarded to specific scientific institutions to undertake particular aspects of research which have been prioritised by the Commission. Their work is done under the supervision of the European Commission.

Direct action

Direct action refers to the research work that is undertaken at the Community's Joint Research Centre in Italy.

Concerted action

The final category consists of that research work which is carried out by Member States in co-operation with non-EC countries.

ACE

Under a Regulation adopted in 1984, funding was provided for a programme of Action relating to the Environment (ACE). The programme ended in 1987 and has been succeeded by another which provides support from 1987–1991. This programme will provide funding for research in the following areas:

- development of 'clean' technologies – that is, those that cause little or no pollution and are also economical in the use of natural resources
- development of techniques for waste recycling and re-use
- development of techniques to locate sites that have been contaminated by hazardous waste and methods of treating them
- development of methods to measure and monitor the quality of the environment
- projects which aim to protect land under threat from erosion, fire or desertification, or methods to reclaim land that has fallen prey to these threats.

STEP and EPOCH

A proposal presented by the Commission in early 1989 proposes that two programmes should receive EC funding for the period 1989–1992:

STEP–Science and Technology for Environmental Protection – ECU 75 million.

EPOCH – European Programme on Climatology and Natural Hazards – ECU 40 million.

STEP is divided into several major research areas including:

- the environment and human health
- the assessment of the risks associated with chemicals
- research into atmospheric processes and air quality
- the quality of water in the Community

- the protection of the soil and of groundwater
- research into ecosystems
- research into new technologies for environmental protection.

EPOCH is mainly concerned with studying the climatic change and the effects that this will have on the environment in the future. It is not the first programme which has concentrated its efforts on climatology as a four-year programme which ended in 1985 had a similar brief.

It is not only the Commission that is providing the thrust for cooperative environmental programmes. For example, corporate concerns in West Germany, France and the United Kingdom have agreed a programme of cooperative research and a pooling of resources to perfect the European Fast Reactor. This is a revolutionary energy saving type of reactor that conserves uranium (thus cutting down on waste) by extracting considerably more energy from it than conventional reactors. The programme is expected to cost in excess of £20 million per year and is being financed by the European Fast Reactor Utilities Group, a grouping of six national electricity authorities.

Individual Member States are also taking certain actions in isolation. For example, in the UK innovations which are aimed at improving pollution control are receiving central government support. In 1988 the Environmental Protection Technology scheme was set up by the Department of the Environment, and approximately £10 million is available over the next four years to help British industry compete in markets where high environmental standards are being imposed. Areas which have been prioritised for action include:

- research into alternatives to CFCs
- research into ways to reduce the emissions from the burning of municipal waste.

What remains to be done?

Research into environmental issues and new technologies to combat existing environmental degradation is an essential complement to a coherent environmental policy. Increasing priority has to be given to such research projects. Lobbyists, including Members of the European Parliament, are putting pressure on the Community to allocate more money to these projects.

Legislative measures

GENERAL PROVISIONS AND PROGRAMMES

86/234/EEC: Council Decision of 10 June 1986 adopting multiannual R & D programmes in the field of the environment (1986 to 1990).
OJ L 159, 14.06.86, p. 31

---

9 International Co-operation

In recent years, the Commission has developed its role in the international arena in recognition of the need for global action to protect the environment.

In the most recent environment programme the Commission established the following priorities in this area:

- strengthening its participation in the Helsinki and Oslo Conventions which protect regional seas
- protecting the Mediterranean through implementing the Genoa Convention
- protecting animals from vivisection by participating in the Council of Europe Convention
- developing legislation to ensure Member States adhere to international agreements on the transport of hazardous chemicals
- working more closely with third countries, in particular, the US, Japan, and the European Free Trade Association (EFTA)
- fully participating in protecting the Third World from exports of dangerous substances.

The Third World deserves particular attention, in that it faces significant threats of desertification, deforestation, over-population and wildlife eradication. The recent concern for the irrecoverable destruction of the tropical rain forests is one example of an increasing problem. The range of actions that the Community is taking to halt this destruction include:

- close scrutiny of every Member State's trade policies and their impact on the tropical rain forests
- financing of conservation projects, in particular through the Euro-

pean Investment Bank
- promoting a voluntary code of conduct aimed at EC-based timber companies. This aims to ensure that timber brought into the Community is sourced from environmentally sound suppliers.

It has been recognised that these issues must be considered not in isolation but rather in the context of international agreements such as the Lomé Convention (which governs trade between the Community and African, Caribbean and Pacific States).

In addition, legislation is being discussed by Member States which will allow the European Commission to negotiate and approve international agreements on behalf of all Member Countries. These agreements are those which specifically relate to regions within the Community that need particular environmental action.

In the future, the Commission will attempt to co-ordinate national development policies across the Community. The role that national representatives should take in organisations such as the World Bank and the Inter-American Development Bank is being considered to ensure that aid funding decisions are increasingly environmentally aware.

The Commission is not alone in recognising the importance of international co-operation in the context of environmental issues. Non-EC countries, national and international voluntary organisations, trade federations and other international groupings are increasingly pressing for international action essential to find global solutions.

International conventions on particular environmental issues are being held with increasing regularity as the immediacy of the problems has increased. Furthermore these forums encourage the exchange of ideas and information.

Legislative measures

INTERNATIONAL COOPERATION

Convention for the Conservation of Salmon in the North Atlantic Ocean.
OJ L 378, 31.12.82, p. 25
O by 382D0886 (OJ L 378, 31.12.82, p. 24)

Protocol for the protection of the Mediterranean Sea against pollution from land-based sources.
OJ L 067, 12.03.83, p. 3
O by 383D0101 (OJ L 067, 12.03.83, p. 1)

Convention on fishing and conservation of the living resources in the Baltic Sea and the Belts.
OJ L 237, 26.08.83, p. 5
M by 283A0826(03) (OJ L 237, 26.08.83, p. 9)
O by 383D0414 (OJ L 237, 26.08.83, p. 4)

Protocol to the Conference of the representatives of the States Parties to the Convention on fishing and conservation of living resources in the Baltic Sea and the Belts (Warsaw, 9 to 11 November 1982).
OJ L 237, 26.08.83, p. 9
O by 383D0414 (OJ L 237, 26.08.83, p. 4)

Exchange of letters between the Commission and the United Nations Environment Programme on the strengthening of cooperation between the two institutions.
OJ C 248, 16.09.83, p. 2

Agreement for cooperation in dealing with pollution of the North Sea by oil and other harmful substances (Bonn Agreement).
OJ L 188, 16.07.84, p. 9
O by 384D0358 (OJ L 188, 16.07.84, p. 7)

Proposal from the International Commission for the Protection of the Rhine against Pollution to supplement Annex IV to the

Convention on the protection of the Rhine against chemical pollution, signed in Bonn on 3 December 1976.
OJ L 175, 05.07.85, p. 37

Protocole d'amendement de la convention pour la prévention de la pollution marine d'origine tellurique – Protocol amending the Convention for the prevention of marine pollution from land-based sources.
OJ L 024, 27.01.87, p. 47
O by 387D0057 (OJ L 024, 27.01.87, p. 46)

Cooperation Agreement between the European Economic Community and the Kingdom of Sweden on research in the field of the recycling and utilisation of waste.
OJ L 276, 07.10.88, p. 12
O by 388D0511 (OJ L 276, 07.10.88, p. 11)

Vienna Convention for the protection of the ozone layer.
OJ L 297, 31.10.88, p. 10
O by 388D0540 (OJ L 297, 31.10.88, p. 8)

Montreal Protocol on substances that deplete the ozone layer.
OJ L 297, 31.10.88, p. 21
O by 388D0540 (OJ L 297, 31.10.88, p. 8)

Community-COST concertation Agreement on seven concerted action projects in the field of the environment.
OJ L 344, 13.12.88, p. 13

75/438/EEC: Council Decision of 3 March 1975 concerning Community participation in the Interim Commission established on the basis of resolution No III of the convention for the prevention of marine pollution from land-based sources.
OJ L 194, 25.07.75, p. 22

Council Resolution of 3 March 1975 on the convention for the prevention of marine pollution from land-based sources.
OJ C 168, 25.07.75, p. 1

76/51/EEC: Commission Recommendation to the Member

States invited to attend the intergovernmental meeting in Barcelona.
OJ L 009, 16.01.76, p. 35

77/586/EEC: Council Decision of 25 July 1977 concluding the Convention for the protection of the Rhine against chemical pollution and an Additional Agreement to the Agreement, signed in Berne on 29 April 1963, concerning the International Commission for the Protection of the Rhine against Pollution.
OJ L 240, 19.09.77, p. 35

80/565/Euratom: Council Decision of 9 June 1980 approving the conclusion by the Commission of the International Convention on the physical protection of nuclear material.
OJ L 149, 17.06.80, p. 41

81/462/EEC: Council Decision of 11 June 1981 on the conclusion of the Convention on long-range transboundary air pollution.
OJ L 171, 27.06.81, p. 11

82/460/EEC: Council Decision of 24 June 1982 on a supplement to Annex IV to the Convention on the protection of the Rhine against chemical pollution.
OJ L 210, 19.07.82 p. 8

85/613/EEC: Council Decision of 20 December 1985 concerning the adoption, on behalf of the Community, of programmes and measures relating to mercury and cadmium discharges under the convention for the prevention of marine pollution from land-based sources.
OJ L 375, 31.12.85, p. 20

86/277/EEC: Council Decision of 12 June 1986 on the conclusion of the Protocol to the 1979 Convention on long-range transboundary air pollution on long-term financing of the cooperative programme for monitoring and evaluation of the long-range transmission of air pollutants in Europe (EMEP).
OJ L 181, 04.07.86, p. 1

88/381/EEC: Council Decision of 24 June 1988 concerning a

supplement, in respect of carbon tetrachloride, to Annex IV to the Convention for the Protection of the Rhine against Chemical Pollution.
OJ L 183, 14.07.88, p. 27

88/540/EEC: Council Decision of 14 October 1988 concerning the conclusion of the Vienna Convention for the protection of the ozone layer and the Montreal Protocol on substances that deplete the ozone layer.
OJ L 297, 31.10.88, p. 8

88/615/EEC: Council Decision of 8 December 1988 concerning the conclusion of a Community-COST concertation Agreement on seven concerted action projects in the field of the environment.
OJ L 344, 13.12.88, p. 12

Convention concerning the International Commission for the Rhine (Berne Convention).
OJ L 240, 19.09.77, p. 48

Convention on international trade in endangered species of wild fauna and flora
OJ L 384, 31.12.82, p. 7
O by 382R3626 (OJ L 384, 31.12.82, p. 1)

Convention on the Prevention of Marine Pollution from land-based sources (Paris Convention).
OJ L 194, 25.07.75, p. 5
M by 287A0127(01) (OJ L 024, 27.01.87, p. 47)
O by 375D0437 (OJ L 194, 25.07.75, p. 5)

Convention on the protection of the Mediterranean Sea against pollution (Barcelona Convention).
OJ L 240, 19.09.77, p. 3
O by 377D0585 (OJ L 240, 19.09.77, p. 1)

Protocol concerning cooperation in combating pollution of the Mediterranean Sea by oil and other harmful substances in cases of emergency.
OJ L 162, 19.06.81, p. 6

O by 381D0420 (OJ L 162, 19.06.81, p. 4)

Convention on the conservation of European wildlife and nat-
ural habitats.
OJ L 038, 10.02.82, p. 3
O by 382D0072 (OJ L 038, 10.02.82, p. 1)

Convention on long-range transboundary air pollution.
OJ L 171, 27.06.81, p. 13
O by 381D0462 (OJ L 171, 27.06.81, p. 11)
M by 386D0277 (OJ L 181, 04.07.86, p. 1)

Convention on the conservation of Antarctic marine living
resources.
OJ L 252, 05.09.81, p. 27
O by 381D0691 (OJ L 252, 05.09.81, p. 26)

10 Implications for business

Companies in the Community which have not placed green issues high on their corporate agenda are now having to consider their impact on the environment. Increasingly, through specific legislation and lobbying environmental issues can have an effect on:

- costs
- employment
- compliance
- monitoring
- investment.

In addition, companies themselves are becoming active in lobbying.

Costs

The appearance of 'environmentally friendly' products on the shelves of supermarkets demonstrates that manufacturers are responding to the demands of the green consumer. However, manufacturers do face cost increases in developing these new products; costs which, in many cases, are passed on to the consumer. However, a recent consumer poll in the UK established that over half of the consumers questioned would be willing to pay 5 per cent more for their purchases if these were environmentally friendly.

Protecting the environment can also save companies money. For example, the switch to lead free petrol in company car has been estimated to save at least £210 per 60 000 miles.

Employment

The Commission is convinced that improving environmental conditions in the Community can increase levels of employment. In 1988, it established a five year project which aims to illustrate this. ECU 33 million has been allocated to this programme. Not only are actions protecting the environment included in this project, but also measures which change harmful practices such as polluting farming methods, certain touristic activities and the wastage of natural resources.

Compliance

Compliance with environmental policy such as reducing noxious emissions from factories may involve completely new production processes requiring significant investment in equipment and staffing. It has been estimated that the cost of complying with reduced sulphur emission levels in factories and power stations will soon reach ECU 1 billion a year.

However, there are also benefits for manufacturers in new EC-wide standards. For example, in the car industry, the harmonisation of exhaust emissions will allow rationalisation of production to one standard to serve the whole of the Community market.

Monitoring

Companies, in the medium term, may be required to undertake monitoring of their activities which may be harmful to the environment and produce regular returns to an EC-wide body such as the European Environment Agency.

Investment

Clearly, the onus is on industry to invest in new 'clean technologies' as preventative measures in addition to the investment required to find new ways of disposing of existing pollutants.

For example, ICI, responding to pressure groups, has agreed to halt the dumping of chemical waste into the North Sea from the early 1990s. Considerable investment will be required to find environmentally acceptable alternatives. This particular company estimates that 25 per cent of the cost of building new plants is accounted for in measures to protect the environment.

Harming the environment can no longer be considered a cost-free means of enhancing a company's return on investment.

Lobbying

Any business which has a view on Community environmental legislation can make its views known during the formative stages of the legislation. Lobbying organisations are very strong, the most powerful being UNICE, an organisation representing the equivalent of the CBIs across Europe. Some feel that direct approaches from companies can also be effective, although Commission officials often prefer to deal with representative organisations. The influence that lobbyists can have on the final form of legislation should not be underestimated and therefore companies should take the opportunity to raise their concerns.

11 Conclusions

The pace of environmental deterioration and its irreversible consequences clearly requires broader action than Commission legislation. Although bringing environmental considerations into planning and development decisions made within the Commission is a clear signal that the agenda is becoming green, there are still many obstacles.

The perception of environmental concerns as being marginal has lead to a lack of resources, both financial and human, within the Commission. In times of economic recession, environmental concerns have had to take a secondary place.

There are abundant problems in developing European environmental policy:

- the varying levels of national commitment across the Community and differing national priorities have very often led to legislation geared to the lowest common denominator rather than to environmentally acceptable standards
- compromises have not only been required to satisfy the 12 Member States. Within Commission departments, compromises have been required to satisfy conflicting priorities.

Despite the difficulties, the Commission is committed to continuing work in this area, believing that there is no choice between environmental protection and economic growth:

The only choice this generation faces is one of recognising and facing up to the responsibilities that all of us share – namely to pass on to our children a world fit to live in and fit to enjoy.

From *European Documentation* ISBN 92-825-7273-0.

Appendix I

Single European Act

Article 25

A Title VII shall be added to Part Three of the EEC Treaty reading as follows:

TITLE VII
ENVIRONMENT

Article 130 R

1 Action by the Community relating to the environment shall have the following objectives:

- to preserve, protect and improve the quality of the environment;
- to contribute towards protecting human health;
- to ensure a prudent and rational utilisation of natural resources.

2 Action by the Community relating to the environment shall be based on the principles that preventive action should be taken, that environmental damage should as a priority be rectified at source, and that the polluter should pay. Environmental protection requirements shall be a component of the Community's other policies.

3 In preparing its action relating to the environment, the Community shall take account of:

- available scientific and technical data;
- environmental conditions in the various regions of the Community;
- the potential benefits and costs of action or of lack of action;
- the economic and social development of the Community as a whole and the balanced development of its regions.

4 The Community shall take action relating to the environment to the extent to which the objectives referred to in paragraph 1 can be attained better at Community level than at the level of the individual Member States. Without prejudice to certain measures of a Community nature, the Member States shall finance and implement the other measures.

5 Within their respective spheres of competence, the Community and the Member States shall co-operate with third countries and with the relevant international organisations. The arrangements for Community co-operation may be the subject of agreements between the Community and the third parties concerned, which shall be negotiated and concluded in accordance with Article 228.

The previous paragraph shall be without prejudice to Member States' competence to negotiate in international bodies and to conclude international agreements.

Article 130 S

The Council, acting unanimously on a proposal from the Commission and after consulting the European Parliament and the Economic and Social Committee, shall decide what action is to be taken by the Community.

The Council shall, under the conditions laid down in the preceding sub-paragraph, define those matters on which decisions are to be taken by a qualified majority.

Article 130 T

The protective measures adopted in common pursuant to Article 130 S shall not prevent any Member State from maintaining or introducing more stringent protective measures compatible with this Treaty.

Appendix II

European Community Directives from Start to Finish

The Consultation Procedure

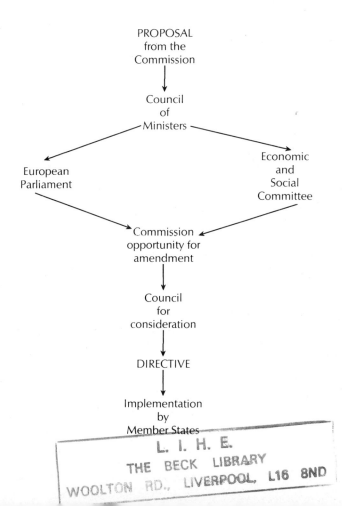

PROPOSAL
from the
Commission

↓

Council
of
Ministers

European
Parliament

Economic
and
Social
Committee

Commission
opportunity for
amendment

↓

Council
for
consideration

↓

DIRECTIVE

↓

Implementation
by
Member States

The Co-operation Procedure

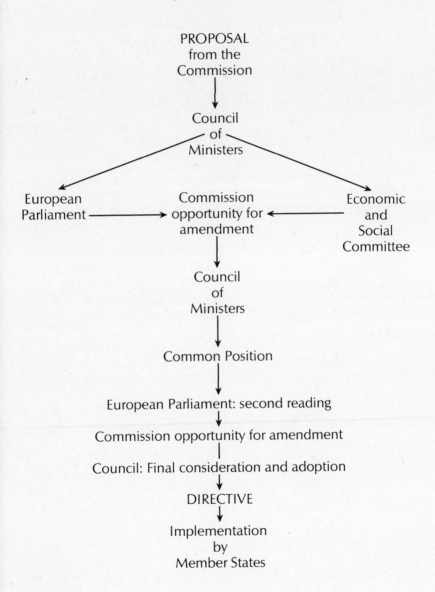

PROPOSAL
from the
Commission

Council
of
Ministers

European   Commission   Economic
Parliament ────────▶ opportunity for ◀──────── and
                                      amendment   Social
                                                                                   Committee

Council
of
Ministers

Common Position

European Parliament: second reading

Commission opportunity for amendment

Council: Final consideration and adoption

DIRECTIVE

Implementation
by
Member States

Appendix III

Organisations

Ark
Press Office
500 Harrow Road
London W9 3QA
Tel: 01 968 6780

**British Trust for Conservation
    Volunteers**
36 St Mary's Street
Wallingford
Oxon OX10 0EU
Tel: 0491 39766

Campaign for Lead Free Air
3 Endsleigh St.
London WC1H 0DD
Tel: 0273 601312

Common Ground
45 Shelton Street
London WC2H 9HJ
Tel: 01 379 3109

**Council for the Protection of
    Rural England (CPRE)**
4 Hobart Place
London SW1W 0HY
Tel: 01 235 9481

**Council for the Protection of
    Rural Wales**
Ty Gwyn
31 High Street
Welshpool
Powys SY21 8JD
Tel: 0938 552525

Countryside Commission
John Dower House
Crescent Place
Cheltenham
Glos GL50 3RA
Tel: 0242 521381

**Countryside Commission for
    Scotland**
Battleby
Redgorton
Perth PH1 3EW
Tel: 0738 27921

The Environment Council
80 York Way
London N1 9AG
Tel: 01 278 4736

Forestry Commission
231 Costorphine Road
Edinburgh EH12 7AT
Tel:031 334 0303

Friends of the Earth
26–28 Underwood Street
London N1 7JQ
Tel: 01 490 1555

Green Party
10 Station Parade
Balham High Road
London SW12
Tel: 01 673 0045

Greenpeace UK
30–31Islington Green
London N1 8XE
Tel: 01 354 5100

**International Union for
Conservation of Nature**
53 The Green
Richmond
Kew,
Surrey TW9 3AA
Tel: 01 940 4547

Irish Wildlife Federation
132a East Wall Road
Dublin 3, Eire
Tel: 0001 366821

Marine Conservation Society
9 Gloucester Road
Ross-on-Wye
Herefordshire HR9 5BU
Tel: 0989 66017

Men of the Trees
Sandy Lane
Crawley Down
West Sussex RH10 4HS
Tel: 0342 712536

**National Centre for Organic
Gardening**
Ryton-on-Dunsmore
Coventry CV8 3LG
Tel: 0203 303517

Nature Conservancy Council
Northminster House
Peterborough PE1 1UA
Tel: 0733 40345

Pond Action
c/o Dept of Biological and
Molecular Sciences
Oxford Polytechnic
Gipsy Lane
Headington
Oxford OX3 0BP
Tel: 0865 819282

Ramblers Association
1–5 Wandsworth Road
London SW8 2XX
Tel: 01 582 6878

**Royal Society for Nature
Conservation (RSNC)**
The Green
Nettleham
Lincoln LN2 2NR
Tel: 0522 752326

**Royal Society for the
Prevention of Cruelty to
Animals (RSPCA)**
The Causeway
Horsham
West Sussex RH12 1H9
Tel: 0403 64181

**Royal Society for the
Protection of Birds (RSPB)**
The Lodge
Sandy
Bedfordshire SG19 2DL
Tel: 0767 80551

Survival International
310 Edgeware Road
London W2 1DY
Tel: 01 723 5535

Transport 2000
Walkden House
10 Melton Street
London NW1 2EJ
Tel: 01 388 8386

**Ulster Society for the
Preservation of the
Countryside**
West Winds
Carney Hill
Craigavad
Holywood
Co. Down BT18 0JR
Tel: 0232 381304

**Women's Environmental
Network**
287 City Road
London EC1V 1LA
Tel: 01 490 2511

Woodland Trust
Autumn Park
Disart Road
Grantham
Lincs NG31 6LL
Tel: 0476 74297

**World Wide Fund for Nature
(WWF)**
Panda House
Weyside Park
Godalming
Surrey GU7 1XR
Tel: 0483 426444

Appendix IV

European Documentation Centres in the UK

The European Documentation Centres are extremely valuable regional sources of information on the Community. Based at Institutes of Higher Education, they all stock the *Official Journal*, which lists all Community tenders as well as copies of draft legislation/Directives. Other important documents relating to many Community aspects can also be found at these centres.

ABERDEEN
The Library
University of Aberdeen
Meston Walk
Aberdeen AB9 2UB
Tel: 0224 40241 x 2787

ASHFORD
Library
Wye College
Wye
Ashford
Kent TN25 5AH
Tel: 0233 812401 x 497

BATH
University Library
University of Bath
Claverton Down
Bath BA2 7AY
Tel: 0225 826826 x 5594

BELFAST
The Library
Government Publications Dept
Queens University
Belfast
Northern Ireland BT7 1LS
Tel: 0232 245133 x 3605

BIRMINGHAM
William Kendrick Library
Birmingham Polytechnic
Birmingham B42 2SU
Tel: 021-331 5289

Main Library
University of Birmingham
PO Box 363
Birmingham B15 2TT
Tel: 021-414 5823

BRADFORD

J. B. Priestley Library
University of Bradford
Richmond Road
Bradford BD7 1DP
Tel: 0274 733466 x 8263

BRIGHTON

The Library
University of Sussex
Brighton BN1 9QL
Tel: 0273 678159

BRISTOL

Law Library
University of Bristol
Queens Road
Bristol BS8 1RJ
Tel: 0272 303370

CAMBRIDGE

The Library
University of Cambridge
West Road
Cambidge CB3 9DR
Tel: 0223 333138

CARDIFF

Arts and Social Studies Library
University College
PO Box 430
Cardiff CF1 3XT
Tel: 0222 8744262

CHALFONT

The Buckinghamshire College
  of Higher Education
Newlands Park
Gorelands Lane
Chalfont St Giles HP8 44D
Tel: 02405 4441 x 245

COLCHESTER

The Library
University of Essex
PO Box 24
Colchester CO4 3UA
Tel: 0206 862286

COLERAINE

The Library
New University of Ulster
Coleraine BT52 1SA
Tel: 0265 4141 x 257

COVENTRY

The Library
Lanchester Polytechnic
Priory Street
Coventry CV1 2HF
Tel: 0203 24166 x 2452/2698

The Library
University of Warwick
Coventry CV4 7A
Tel: 0203 523523 x 2041

DUNDEE

University of Dundee
Perth Road
Dundee DD1 4HN
Tel: 0382 23181 x 4101

DURHAM

Official Publications Section
University Library
Stockton Road
Durham DH1 3LY
Tel: 091-374 3041

EDINBURGH
Centre of European
    Government Studies
University of Edinburgh
Old College
South Bridge
Edinburgh EH8 9LY
Tel: 031-667 1011 x 4215

ESSEX
Essex Institute of Higher
    Education
Victoria Road South
Chelmsford
Essex CM1 1LL
Tel: 0245 493131

EXETER
Centre for European Legal
    Studies
Exeter Building (Law Faculty)
Amory Building
Rennes Drive
Exeter EX4 4RJ
Tel: 0392 263356

GLASGOW
The University Library
University of Glasgow
Hillhead Street
Glasgow G12 9QE
Tel: 041-339 8855 x 6744

GUILDFORD
George Edwards Library
University of Surrey
Guildford GU2 5XH
Tel: 0483 509233

HULL
Brynmor Jones Library
University of Hull
Cottingham Road
Hull HU6 7RX
Tel: 0482 465441

KEELE
The Library
University of Keele
Keele
Staffs ST5 5RG
Tel: 0782 621111 x 3737

KENT
Library Building
University of Kent
Canterbury
Kent CT2 7NU
Tel: 0227 66822

LANCASTER
University of Lancaster Library
Lancaster LA1 4YX
Tel: 0524 65201 x 276

LEEDS
The Library
Leeds Polytechnic
Calverley Street
Leeds LS1 3HE
Tel: 0532 462925

University of Leeds
20 Lyddon Terrace
Leeds LS7 9JT
Tel: 0532 31751

LEICESTER
University Library
University of Leicester
University Road
Leicester LE1 7RH
Tel: 0533 522044

LIVERPOOL
Liverpool and District Science
  and Industry Research
  Council
Central Libraries
William Brown Street
Liverpool L3 8EW
Tel: 051-207 2147 x 45

LONDON
The Library
Queen Mary College
Mile End Road
London E1 4NS
Tel: 01-980 4811 x 3307

The Library
Polytechnic of North London
Prince of Wales Road
London NW5
Tel: 01-359 0941

British Library
English Collection
Great Russell Street
London WC1B 3DB
Tel: 01-323 7602

The Library
R11A
10 St James Square
London SW1Y 4LE
Tel: 01-930 2233 x 260

European Depository Library
Central Reference Library
City of Westminster Library
St Martin's Street
London WC2 7HP
Tel: 01-798 3131

British Library of Political and
  Economic Science
The Library
10 Portugal Street
London WC2A 2HD
Tel: 01-405 7686 x 2993

LOUGHBOROUGH
The Library
Loughborough University of
  Technology
Loughborough LE11 3TU
Tel: 0509 222344

MANCHESTER
John Rylands Library
University of Manchester
Oxford Road
Manchester M13 9PP
Tel: 061-273 3333

NEWCASTLE-UPON-TYNE
The Library
Newcastle Polytechnic
Ellison Place
Newcastle-upon-Tyne NE1 8ST
Tel: 091-275 3727

NORWICH
The Library
University of East Anglia
University Plain
Norwich NR4 7TJ
Tel: 0603 56161 x 2412

NOTTINGHAM
The Library
University of Nottingham
Nottingham NG7 2RD
Tel: 0602 506101 x 3741

OXFORD
Bodleian Library
University of Oxford
Oxford OX1 3BG
Tel: 0865 277201

PORTSMOUTH
Frewen Library
Portsmouth Polytechnic
Cambridge Road
Portsmouth PO1 2ST
Tel: 0705 277201

READING
The Library
University of Reading
Whiteknights
PO Box 223
Reading RG6 2AH
Tel: 0734 874331 x 131

SALFORD
The Library
University of Salford
Salford M5 4WT
Tel: 061 736 5843 x 7218

SHEFFIELD
The Library
Sheffield City Polytechnic
Pond Street
Sheffield S1 1WB
Tel: 0742 20911 x 2494

SOUTHAMPTON
Faculty of Law
University of Southampton
Southampton SO9 5NH
Tel: 0703 559122 x 3451

WESTERBY
British Library
Document Supply Centre
Boston Spa
Westerby LS23 7BQ
Tel: 0937 843434 x 6035

WOLVERHAMPTON
Robert Scott Library
Polytechnic of Wolverhampton
St Peter's Square
Wolverhampton WV1 1RH
Tel: 0902 313005 x 2300

Appendix V
Other Sources of Information

Catherine Taylor, one of the authors, can be contacted at:

The Marketing Shop
18 Kingly Court
London W1R 5LE
Tel: 01-434 2671

General information on EC matters can be obtained from the Commission's UK offices.

These are found at:

8 Storey's Gate
London SW1P 3AT
Tel: 01-222 8122

Windsor House
9–15 Bedford Street
Belfast BT2 7EG
Tel: 0232 40708

4 Cathedral Road
Cardiff CF1 9JG
Tel: 0222 37 1631

7 Alva Street
Edinburgh EH2 4PH
Tel: 031 225 2058